Romantic Appliqué

MILNER CRAFT SERIES

Romantic Appliqué

Yvonne Overton

SALLY MILNER PUBLISHING

First published in 1994 by
Sally Milner Publishing Pty Ltd
at 'The Pines'
RMB 54 Burra Road
Burra Creek NSW 2620

Reprinted 1995, 1996

© Yvonne Overton 1994

Design by Shirley Peters
Photography by Andrew Elton
Styling by Lisa Hilton
Typeset by Asset Typesetting Pty Ltd
Printed in Australia by Impact Printing

National Library of Australia
Cataloguing-in-Publication data:

Overton, Yvonne.
    Romantic applique.

    ISBN 1 86351 140 7.

    1. Appliqué – Patterns. 2. Quilts – Patterns. I. Title. (Series:
Milner craft series).

746.445041

PHOTOGRAPHY CREDITS:
Two cushions: Chair from Cane & Cottage. Hat Box: Pearls from the
Mosman Antique Centre. Firescreen: Lamp and cushion from Home &
Garden; Floral wreath and rug from Sandy de Beyer. Bed: Bed linen
from Bed Bath n' Table; Lamp from Home & Garden; Cup and saucer
from Sandy de Beyer.

CONTENTS

ACKNOWLEDGEMENTS

I would like to thank the many people who have helped to make this book possible, in particular my husband and sons for their encouragement and for freeing me from farming and domestic obligations; my friends belonging to Moree Quilters, for their enthusiasm and considered opinions; Patrick Smith for the framing of the picture (see colour pages) and Goodwood Furniture Company for the firescreen frame.

FOREWORD

It is said in American folklore that if you were given an appliquéd quilt to sleep under 'you were indeed an honoured guest'. I think this still holds true today as a hand-appliquéd quilt is very special for several reasons. Firstly, it cannot be made in a day; more likely it would take months or maybe years. Secondly, no other technique has the same appearance of softness and depth as hand appliqué. Because of these facts, hand-appliquéd quilts are generally made for beauty more than for a purely practical use. Appliqué can be worked on many useful, as well as decorative articles around the home.

This book is a result of requests from many people to borrow or buy my patterns used in several quilts. After 25 years of teaching in Technical Colleges of New South Wales, Australia, and conducting many private classes, I realised many women have exceptional needlework skills but don't have the confidence to draw up their own designs. This book is based on one quilt called *Romantically Inclined* and is essentially a pattern book of designs used in this quilt. Each design is complete in itself, so each can be used individually for small projects as shown, or several can be combined in different settings to make an entirely new quilt.

No matter what level of skill you have, with practice you will improve. The best practice is to actually make something, whether it be a cushion, picture, or an entire quilt, while at the same time enjoying the relaxation and pleasure from the making process as much as the completed article.

I hope you find my designs challenging and satisfying.

CHAPTER ONE

FABRIC

One hundred per cent cotton is the ideal fabric for all hand appliqué work, whether a quilt, cushion or picture. Because the cotton is evenly woven, it holds its shape and therefore it is easier to work with.

Polyester cottons (synthetics) are often softer to handle, and hence difficult to work with as they wrinkle along the sewing line.

If the designs are to be used for a cushion or picture, silks are beautiful to use but be wary of some Indian slub silks as they fray very quickly. Usually a wider seam allowance is necessary for all silks.

Whatever the choice of fabric, it should be prewashed to prevent shrinkage and dye loss.

CHAPTER TWO

EQUIPMENT

You need:
- Background fabric. Buy the whole amount at the same time as another roll is often a different dye lot.
- Lots and lots of small pieces of fabric in the desired colour range.
- Threads to match the coloured appliquéd pieces.
- Embroidery thread for stamens and fine stems.
- No. 10 or No. 12 appliqué needles (appliqué needles are slightly longer than a quilting needle). I use lots of needles already threaded in the colours I am using as it saves a lot of threading and unthreading.
- Small scissors to cut fabric and paper.
- B pencil (soft lead) or dressmaker's carbon (sometimes called dressmaker's tracing paper, which comes in different colours) to transfer the design.
- White paper and a fine black marking pen to trace off the design and then use as the pattern.
- A few pins.
- A small plastic bag to hold all the tiny scraps of paper, fabric and threads.

CHAPTER THREE

COLOUR

The selection of colour is a very personal thing. I like to use colours that are side by side on the colour wheel as they always blend harmoniously. The following suggestions might help anyone who hesitates.

- All designs must contain light, medium and dark colour values.
- Tone on tone fabrics are often easier to blend than lots of multi-coloured prints.
- The big multi-coloured prints are wonderful to give texture to the design.
- Look at the wrong side of a fabric as often it is just the colour you need.
- If using a very dark background, the appliqué often has to be brighter in colour than for a light background.
- If pale colours are used on a dark background be careful that the turnings don't show through.
- As leaves make up a large part of the designs, have as many different shades of green as possible. If using mainly blue-greens, as lots of greens are, use a yellow-green or olive occasionally to add a spark.
- Buds, tiny leaves and fine stems are a good opportunity to use the very dark colours without them becoming overpowering.
- Each bouquet can have its own colour scheme or all the bouquets can be co-ordinated, but do keep the flowers somewhere near their true colours.
- Each bouquet must have a focal point and colour is the only way to achieve this. In my designs, it is generally a rose somewhere near the bow.
- Try to balance the flower colours so that each flower stands out. For example, a rose could have the outside row of petals pale with the centre dark, next to a darker rose with a light centre.
- Count the number of petals in a flower, select that number of fabrics, and arrange them in a circle in your hand in a pleasant combination before beginning to sew.

- The bows and ribbons can be used to set the overall colour scheme of the design, even though that particular colour may not be used again.
- To balance the prints of the flowers, I use plain fabrics for the ribbons and bows, using two values of the same colour, but not too close together as from a distance the eye blends them and you don't see the twists and turns of the ribbons.
- If the design has a bow and ribbons, plan the position of the light and dark value/tones alternately around the loops and tails and mark these on your pattern as each ribbon must be distinct.

CHAPTER FOUR

TRANSFERRING THE DESIGN

The designs are drawn full-scale but some are subdivided into two sections. To draw up the complete design, trace out one section plus the centre lines and match up the centre line on the next section and trace off. Continue until the design is complete. Use a white paper and a fine black marking pen.

If the project contains more than one piece of background fabric (for example, a pair of cushions) cut out all the pieces at the same time as they are more likely to be the same size than if cut weeks apart.

The method of transferring the design to the fabric is dependent on the colour of the background fabric.

TRANSFERRING ONTO LIGHT BACKGROUNDS

Fasten the white paper tracing onto a flat surface with adhesive tape. Align the centre of the fabric with the centre of the design. Fasten the fabric down, right side up, with adhesive tape.

With a sharp B pencil (soft lead) very lightly draw the design onto the background fabric, carefully following the lines exactly with a continuous stroke not a feathered one.

If the fabric is not translucent enough, a light-box or a sheet of glass with a light underneath may be used.

TRANSFERRING ONTO DARK BACKGROUNDS

Fasten the background fabric, right side up, onto a flat surface with adhesive tape.

Place a dressmaker's carbon on top with the carbon side facing the background fabric. Dressmaker's carbon comes in red, yellow, blue and white, test which colour is clearest on a scrap of fabric before using.

Place the white paper tracing over the top of the carbon and trace the design with a ballpoint pen, again using a continuous stroke.

As you are tracing out the design, study the order of sewing. Any section under another must be sewn on first — usually buds, stems, then leaves before flowers and bows.

When the whole design is traced onto the fabric you are ready to sew, with the white paper tracing to be used as the pattern and the original in the book for reference.

CHAPTER FIVE

APPLIQUÉ TECHNIQUES

Beautiful appliqué is made up of flowing designs with smooth curves, sharp points and precise piecing, and by following the drawn shape exactly. Subtle little curves are important as they give lightness and life to the design.

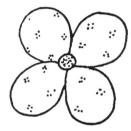 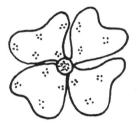

The needleturn method of slip-hemming is used for sewing all the designs as it is the easiest and quickest method once the technique is mastered. On very tight curves and sharp points a tiny hemming stitch is also used.

TO BEGIN APPLIQUÉING

Each petal and leaf is cut out separately in different colours. Select a single leaf from your overall design and cut out the pattern; then cut the leaf out in fabric with about 5 mm (¹⁄₅″) allowance all around.

Position the fabric leaf over the traced leaf on the background fabric. Using the paper pattern as a guide, make sure the allowance is even all around as it is very easy to turn under too much on one side and have nothing left for the other side.

THE NEEDLETURN METHOD OF SLIP-HEMMING

Commence stitching at the top, or 12 o'clock position, of the leaf preferably at a straight section with a knot in the background fabric. Right-handed people stitch from right to left whereas left-handed people stitch from left to right.

Hold the leaf and background fabric firmly between the thumb and forefinger. With the needle tuck under about 4 mm (⅙″) of the turnings until the pencil or carbon line is just covered.

Directly opposite the knot in the background fabric, insert the needle into the fold and run the needle along the fold for about 3 mm (⅛″), bringing the needle out on the back side of the fold.

A small stitch of equal length is then made in the background fabric, commencing opposite the thread from the fold.

With practice, these two stitches can be done in the one movement. The thread must be pulled quite firmly as the thread in the fold holds the edge of the appliqué smoothly onto the background fabric and the stitch should be virtually invisible.

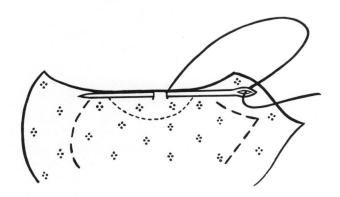

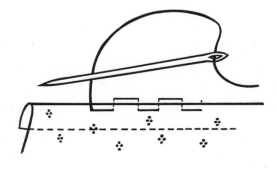

OUTWARD CURVES

Outward curves must be smooth curves. To achieve a flowing line, tuck under only a tiny section at a time. Pivot the needle so that the point sweeps in a wide arc under the leaf. This evens out the pleats in the turnings and gives an even curve.

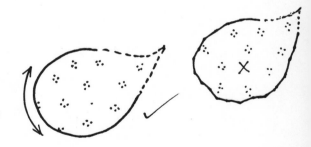

9

For some very tight outward curves it is better to tuck under more than 4 mm (⅙″) allowance and gradually tease the turnings out until the guide line is covered.

POINTS

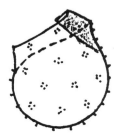 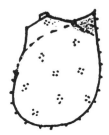

Stitching around a point often causes problems. Firstly, stitch right up to the point and do one tiny hemming stitch on the point. Fold under the turning straight across the point and then fold under again until the design line is just covered. Do one more hemming stitch at the point and continue slip-hemming.

INWARD CURVES

 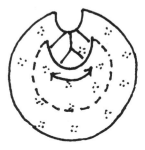

Gentle inward curves cause no problems, but if they are short and sharp the turnings may have to be clipped to allow them to turn under smoothly. Small hemming stitches are often best in these areas.

INWARD CORNERS

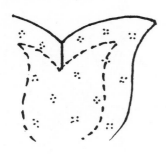 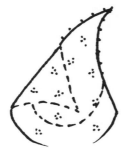

Very sharp inward corners are very difficult to do. It is much better to divide the leaf or petal into two sections rather than do a clumsy inward corner.

For open inward corners, nick the turnings right into the point and fold under the one side of the corner. Stitch down the first side to the point. Add a few tight hemming stitches to strengthen this weak section. Fold under the second side and ease out until the traced line is just covered and continue stitching.

STEMS

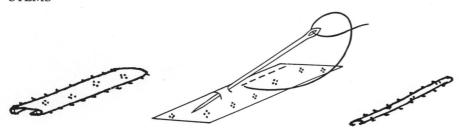

Stems can be sewn on in two ways. For the wide stems, each side can be needleturned and hemmed. If the stem is very narrow, the best method is to sew one side of the stem, with the right side of the stem fabric face down, with a small running stitch. Roll the fabric over to the right side and needleturn and hem the other side.

LONG FINE TAPERS

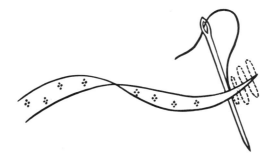

After stitching as for a normal point, with a separate thread, weave backwards and forwards under the sewn appliqué, pulling the thread very tightly. This pulls the sides of the appliqué fabric together and therefore makes it finer and stronger.

BERRY CENTRES

Cut a circular piece of fabric about 4 cm (1⅗″) in diameter and stitch with a double thread around the outside edge and pull it up to fit the centre of the fabric circle. Repeat the process, with the next row of stitching through the outside folded edge. Pull up the thread again, work into a ball and stitch firmly across the back. Finish this thread off and use another to attach to the appliqué.

RIBBONS

As the ribbon twists and changes colour the points must meet. It is best to stitch one section of the ribbon on first and then sew the next colour section on, commencing at the point that touches. Fold straight across the point and fine hem stitch into position. Then hem down one side and back up to finish at the point.

OVERLAPPING PETALS AND LEAVES

If there are a group of petals or leaves together, some will be underneath others. Work out which piece must be sewn on first. As all pieces are cut with a 4 mm turning, only the sections that can be seen are slip hemmed. The sections under another leaf or petal are anchored with a small running stitch. The running stitch is worked close to the outside edge of the turning, to make sure it is not seen when the overlapping leaf is sewn on.

STAMENS AND STEMS — EMBROIDERY

Very little and very basic embroidery stitches are used in the designs. They are only used where appliqué cannot achieve the fineness and definition needed for stamens and stems. One strand of embroidery thread is used for the stitches below.

STRAIGHT STITCH

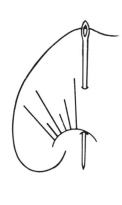

STEM STITCH

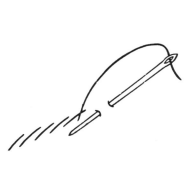

FRENCH KNOTS

BULLION STITCH

CHAPTER SIX

THE PATTERNS

All the patterns are drawn full scale but some are subdivided into two sections. Leaves are all drawn with a centre line in order to differentiate between leaves and petals. The dotted line shown in each pattern indicates the centre both ways.

Correa and Rose Bouquet

Pansy and Rose Bouquet

Geraldton Wax and Rose Bouquet

Foxglove and Rose Bouquet

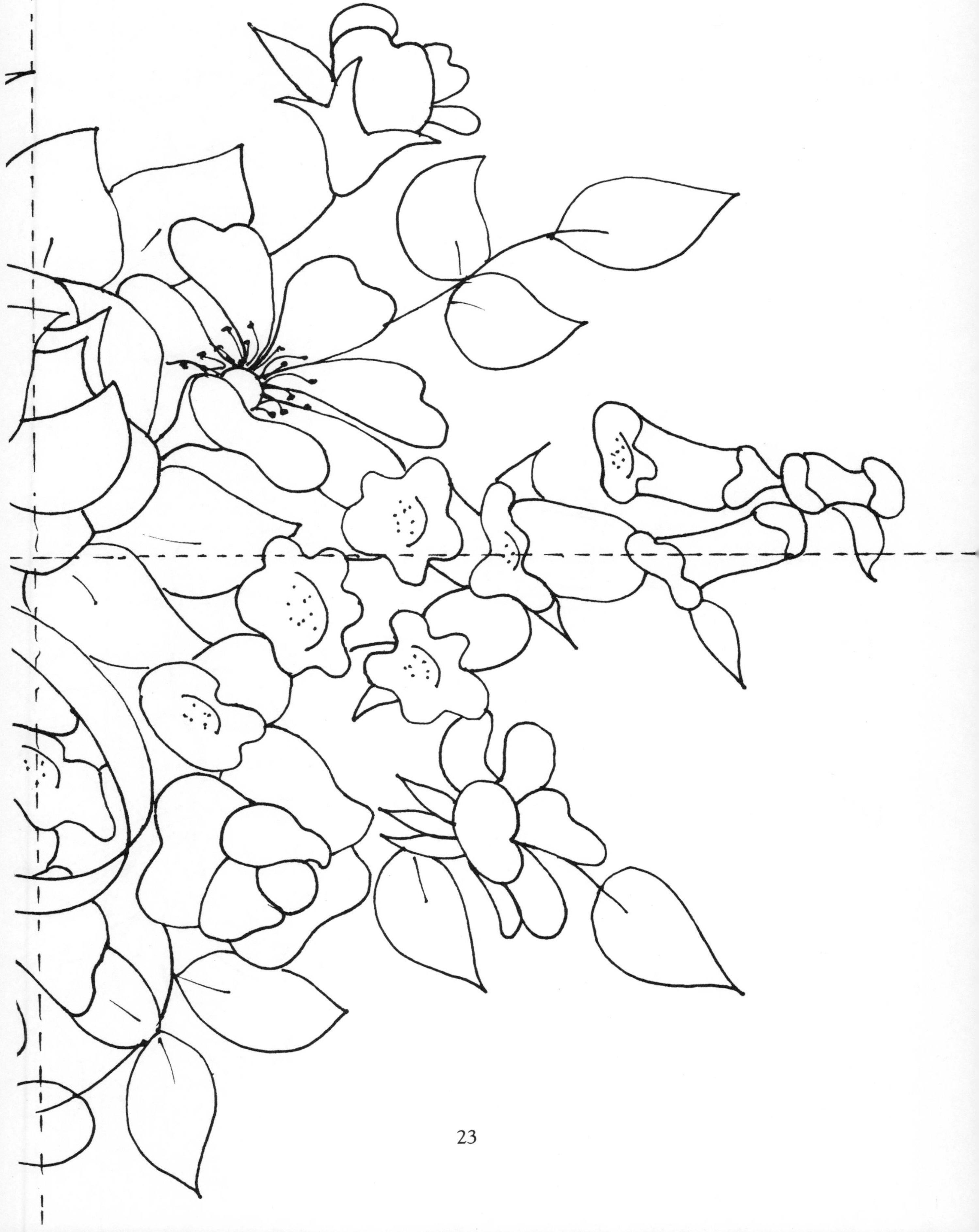

Double Daisy and Rose Bouquet

25

Fuchsia and Rose Bouquet

27

Rose Myrtle and Rose Bouquet

Iris and Rose Bouquet

Ixia and Rose Bouquet

Corner Design

Bow Designs

Scallop Designs

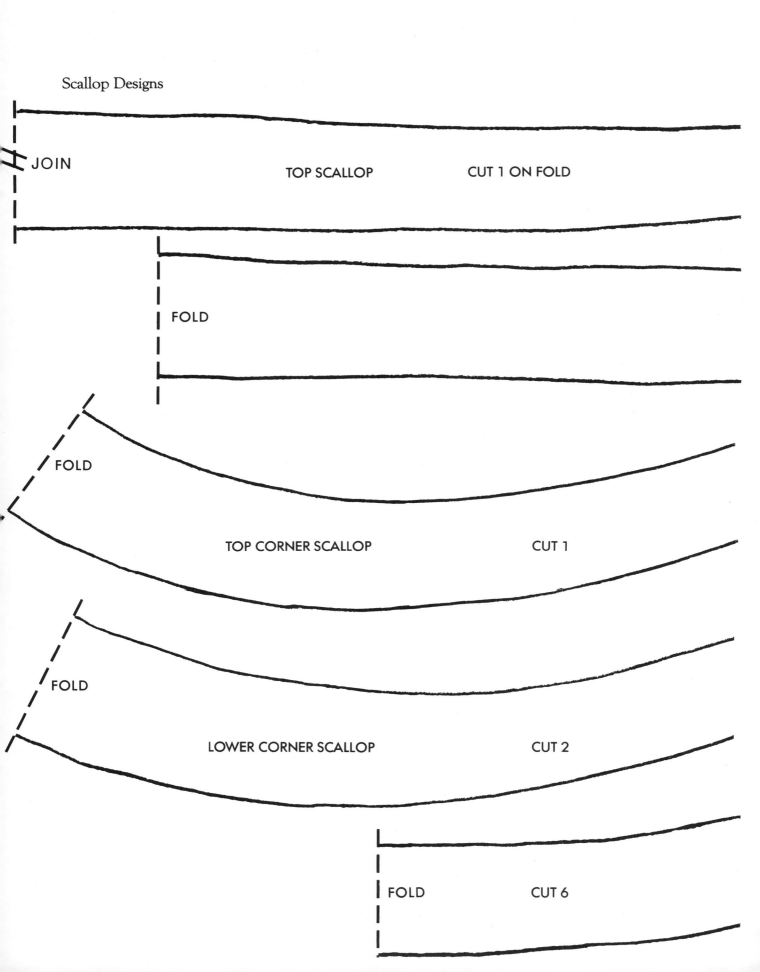

JOIN

TOP SCALLOP   CUT 1 ON FOLD

FOLD

FOLD

TOP CORNER SCALLOP   CUT 1

FOLD

LOWER CORNER SCALLOP   CUT 2

FOLD   CUT 6

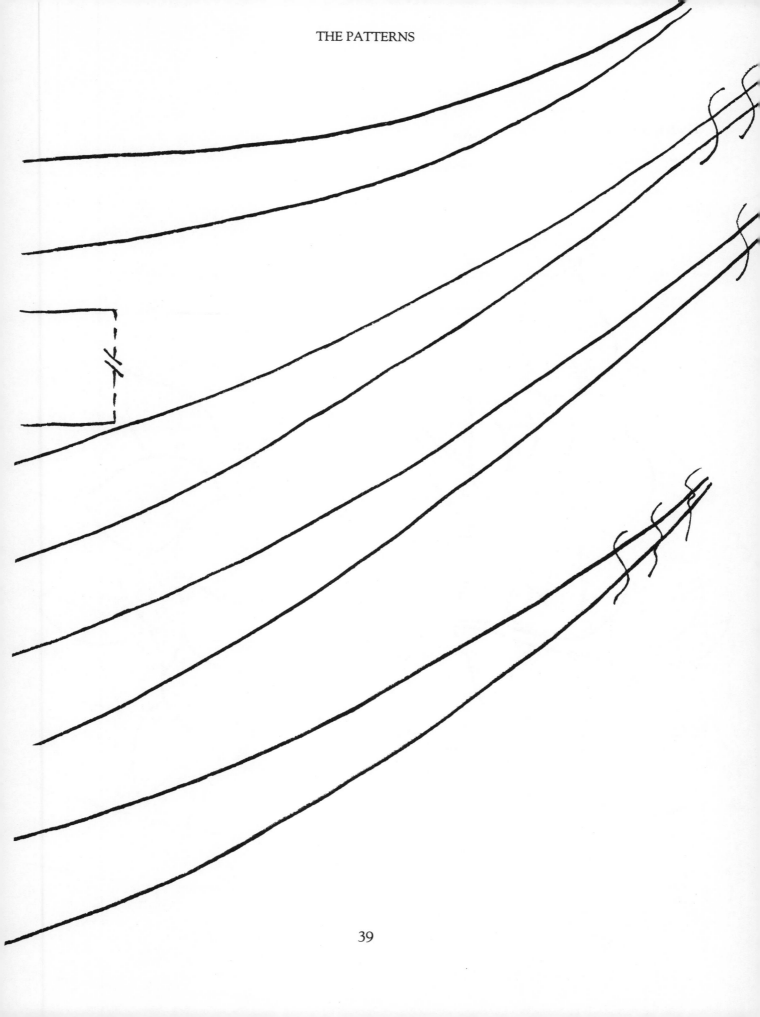

Design for Covered Box

Design for Framed Picture

Design for Side-panel of Firescreen

COVERED BOX

This is an ideal introductory project, with a simple yet attractive design on the padded lid. The background fabric rolls over the top edge and is finished with a wide ribbon that highlights the colours of the appliquéd flowers.

REQUIREMENTS

- Purchased box.
- Background fabric.
- Small pieces of printed fabrics for flowers.
- Green fabrics, varying in tones.
- Threads to match fabrics.
- Wide ribbon — the length around the box.
- Wadding (padding) — the size of the lid.
- Spray glue.

METHOD

1. Measure the lid, add 10–15 cm (4–6″) and cut out background fabric.

2. Transfer design illustrated on page 40 onto background fabric, using the most suitable method. (As suggested in the chapter, Transferring the Design.)

3. Work appliqué as suggested in the chapter Appliqué Techniques (page 8).

4. Cut out wadding (padding) to the size of the lid.

5. Spray glue the lid and fix the wadding into position.

6. Iron appliqué from the back.

7. Spray glue the rim of the lid.

8. Centre the appliqué in the centre of the lid.

9. Ease the background fabric over the top edge and down onto the rim; try to avoid big pleats as they may show through the ribbon.

10. Trim the background to about halfway down the rim.

11. Spray glue the ribbon and wrap it firmly around the rim, covering the cut edge of the background fabric.

THE QUILT —
ROMANTICALLY INCLINED

There are five stages of making the quilt *Romantically Inclined*. To begin, you should do all the appliqué work first. The top sheet is then assembled, after which the scallops and bows are sewn on. You then need to draw the quilting design on the top sheet. Finally, the top sheet wadding (padding) and backing fabric are sewn together by quilting the design drawn on the top sheet.

This quilt was made to fit a 100-year-old bed. Today's bed sizes are many and varied, so the sizes given in the Top Sheet Plan may need to be varied to suit your bed. The side, top and bottom panels surrounding the wreath block can easily be made smaller or larger. If this is done, then the strips between the bouquet blocks will have to be changed also.

REQUIREMENTS

- Background or top sheet fabric (see measurements on following page).
- Lots and lots of small pieces of printed fabrics for the appliqués.
- Wadding/padding to fit the finished size of the top sheet.
- Backing fabric.
- Three different values of the one colour, two for the bows and ribbons and one for the scallops.
- Threads to match the appliqué fabrics.

APPLIQUÉ

To begin, you need to appliqué the wreath for the central block of the top sheet first. Secondly, there are nine separate bouquets to appliqué. Take the measurements for the background fabrics from the Top Sheet Plan (on the following page); remember seam allowance must be added.

METHOD

1. Transfer designs illustrated on the pattern sheet onto background fabrics by the most suitable method. (As suggested in the chapter, Transferring the Design, page 6.)

2. Work appliqué as suggested in the chapter Appliqué Techniques (page 8).

45

TOP SHEET PLAN

The measurements given are finished sizes, so seam allowance must be added.

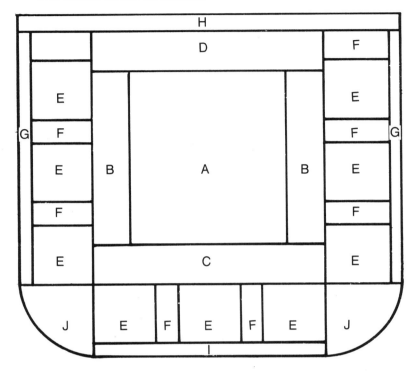

Overall size 271 cm x 223 cm (108²⁄₅″ x 89¹⁄₅″)
A. Central block 104 cm x 82 cm (41³⁄₅″ x 32⁴⁄₅″)
B. Side panels 104 cm x 30 cm (41³⁄₅″ x 12″)
C. Bottom panel 30 cm x 164 cm (12″ x 65³⁄₅″)
D. Top panel 40 cm x 164 cm (16″ x 65³⁄₅″)
E. Appliqué blocks 38 cm x 38 cm (15¹⁄₅″ x 15¹⁄₅″)
F. Strips between blocks 9 cm x 38 cm
    (3³⁄₅″ x 15¹⁄₅″)
G. Side edge strip 174 cm x 9 cm (69³⁄₅″ x 3³⁄₅″)
H. Top edge strip 12 cm x 271 cm (4⁴⁄₅″ x 108²⁄₅″)
I. Lower edge strip 9 cm x 143 cm (3³⁄₅″ x 57¹⁄₅″)
J. Lower corner 47 cm radius (18⁴⁄₅″)

ASSEMBLAGE OF TOP SHEET

Use a sewing machine to assemble. Use the Top Sheet Plan as a guide (above) and follow the step-by-step illustrated instructions listed below.

METHOD

1. Sew side panels to centre block.

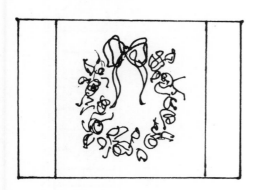

2. Sew top and lower panels to central panel.

3. Join strips between appliquéd blocks.

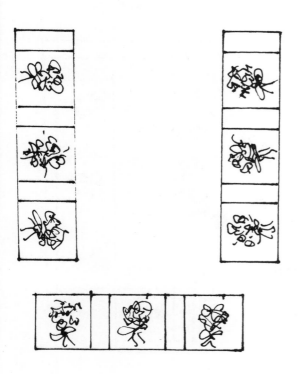

4. Sew outside strips onto appliqué sections.

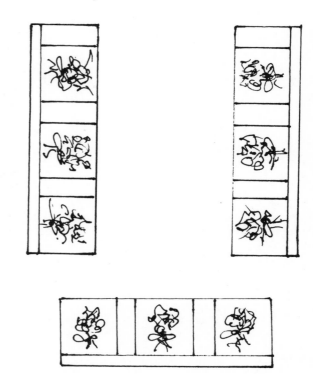

5. Join the lower corners onto the side sections.

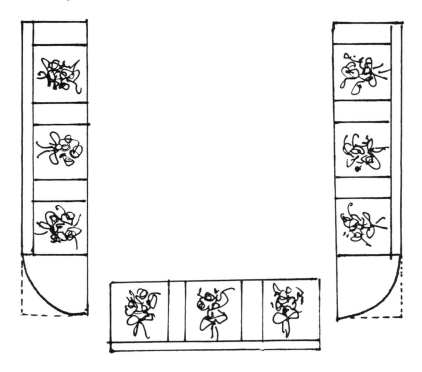

6. Machine lower and side sections to the central section and lastly, sew the strip across the top.

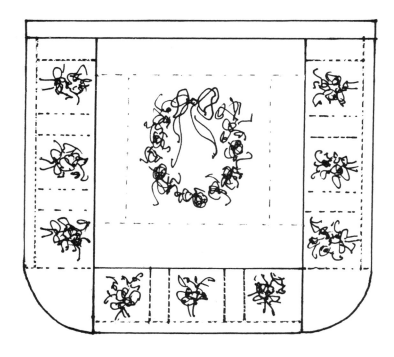

SCALLOPS AND BOWS

Scallops and bows are sewn on after the top sheet is together. The position of the scallop at the base is at the seam junction between the bouquets. Because each bouquet is different, each scallop will be of a different length.

Position of lower side and corner scallops.

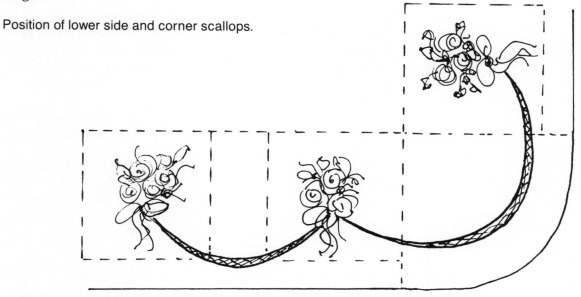

Position of top scallops and bows.

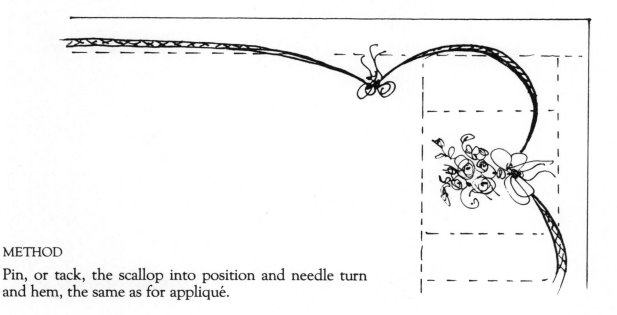

METHOD

Pin, or tack, the scallop into position and needle turn and hem, the same as for appliqué.

DRAWING THE QUILTING DESIGN
ON THE TOP SHEET

Quilting is a technique that uses running stitches to make an interesting pattern while securing the wadding (padding) between the top sheet and backing fabric. It is an essential part of all quilts. Therefore, it is very important that the design be traced very lightly and accurately onto the top sheet with a B lead pencil. As the quilting design is superimposed over the appliqué designs, the two must complement each other. The quilting design for *Romantically Inclined* is made up of several components.

Crosshatching (of 3 mm spacing) is used inside the wreath and again beyond the scallops to the outside edge.

A ring of cable and roses (see pattern sheets at the back of the book) is traced onto the plain areas of the inner panels. The cable and rose quilting pattern supplied is a quarter of the whole. It must be reversed and mirror-imaged to achieve the whole design.

Radiating lines fill in the remaining areas. They radiate from the centre through a 2 cm (⁴⁄₅″) point marked at the outside of the wreath. The lines are taken from the 2 cm (⁴⁄₅″) point to the cable and rose section, then on again until meeting with either the scallops or bouquets.

The appliquéd pieces may be outline quilted, that is, just on the edge of the flowers or leaves but not through the appliquéd fabric. Highlights may also be quilted on the flowers or leaves if desired.

QUILTING

The last stage in the assemblage of the quilt is the quilting — the sewing together of all three layers from the pattern drawn on the top sheet. This is done by hand as I feel machine quilting would detract from the softness and texture of the quilt.

REQUIREMENTS

- Thimble.
- Safety pins.
- Quilting needles.
- Quilting thread.
- A hoop or floor frame.

METHOD

1. The backing fabric, wadding (padding) and the top sheet are safety pinned together at approximately 12–15 cm (4⁴⁄₅″–6″) apart.

2. Work the quilting from the centre to the outside, on a hoop or floor frame, using quilting needles and thread.

3. The work is commenced with a knot on the right side of the quilt, which is popped through the top sheet, to anchor in the wadding (padding).

4. The stitch is made by a rocking action, with the needle pivoting from a thimble on the middle finger, through all three layers until it touches the finger of the underhand. This finger forces the point of the needle up so that a small even stitch is the result.

5. To finish the thread, tie a knot and run it down into the wadding to anchor it.

FINISHING

When the quilting is finished, a bias binding, made with background fabric, is sewn onto the outside edge. If pencil quilting lines were very lightly drawn, they will have worn away by the time the quilt is finished. If not, carefully hand or gentle machine wash with pure soap, rather than harsh detergent. Finally, name, sign and date your quilt as it will become a family heirloom.

COVERED BOX

DETAIL

THE QUILT ROMANTICALLY INCLINED

FRAMED PICTURE

DETAIL OF BOUQUET FROM QUILT

THE TWO CUSHIONS

DETAIL OF
FIRESCREEN
PANEL

FIRESCREEN

FRAMED PICTURE

This is just to show that any of the designs can be used for a picture. The one pictured was worked on a highly polished cotton fabric. Always prewash a polished cotton, even for a picture. With water you lose some of the polish; so if it is not prewashed, the background will mark when dampening the piece to iron before framing. This picture was commercially framed.

REQUIREMENTS

- Background fabric.
- Small pieces of printed fabrics for flower and leaves.
- Two values of one colour for ribbons.
- Thread to match appliqué fabrics.

METHOD

1. Trace the appliqué design from the pattern section (page 41) onto background fabric.

2. Work appliqué as suggested in the chapter Appliqué Techniques (page 8).

3. Iron appliqué from back.
4. Frame.

CUSHIONS

Cushions have always been the most popular small project for appliqué work. They are quick and easy to make and wonderful as a decorative accessory to any home. Two cushions are illustrated (see colour pages). One cushion uses a bouquet design, to show that any of the bouquet blocks from the quilt can be successfully made into cushions, and the other is a corner design (page 34), which would be good for a beginner to try.

Cushions can be made in any size and shape, but generally they are square, and 35 cm (14″) is an average finished size. The insert, which can be made or bought, must be 3 cm (¹⁄₅″) bigger than the cover to give a firm well-filled appearance. Three different edge finishes are described. The piped edge can be used alone or in conjunction with the frill or ruche.

REQUIREMENTS

- Two pieces of fabric cut to required size, 35 cm x 35 cm (14″ x 14″) + seam allowance.
- One strip of same fabric for zip, 35 cm x 5 cm (14″ x 2″) + seam allowance.
- Small pieces of printed fabrics for flower and leaves.
- Two values of one colour for bows.
- Thread to match appliqué fabrics.
- One zip 35 cm (14″).
- Insert for cushion.

METHOD

1. Cut out fabric for cushion.

2. Choose design and transfer it to the fabric as described in the chapter Transferring the Design (page 6).

3. Work appliqué as shown in the chapter Appliqué Techniques (page 8).

4. Insert a zip. The following method of inserting a zip into a cushion eliminates the difficulties of setting the zip onto the ruched, or frilled, side of the cushion.
    — Place zip face down onto the edge of the right side of the narrow strip.

— Machine sew close to the teeth using a zip foot.

— Press seam allowance back so that the zip can be seen.

— On the plain square, fold edge under 2 cm ($^4/_5$″) and iron.

— Pin this folded edge on to machined seam, over the top of the zip.

— Machine a straight line, parallel to and 1.5 cm ($^3/_5$″) from the folded edge.

— As the back of the cushion square is now longer than the appliquéd front, recut the back to the same size as the front, cutting off the excess on the opposite side to the zip. Front and back of the cushion must be the same size, with the zip set in the back.

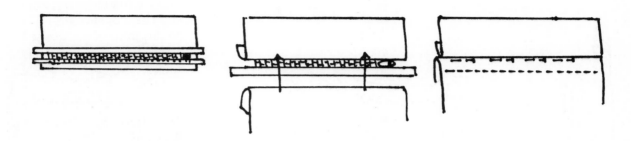

5. Edging — depending on what type you choose, piping, frilling or ruching, you may need a bias strip.

To Cut a Bias Strip

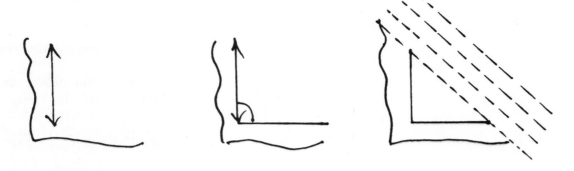

Find the straight grain of the fabric. From a point along that straight grain-line, measure an equal amount up and at right angles to the line. The true bias is found by connecting these two points together. Everything parallel to this diagonal line will be on the true bias.

To Join a Bias Strip

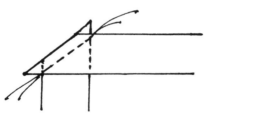

Place two bias strips, right sides together, to form a right angle. Then slide the top strip down until a right angle shows as one edge extends beyond the other. Machine from one right angle to the other right angle and press open. The joined bias should be a continuous, smooth strip.

To Pipe Edge

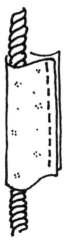

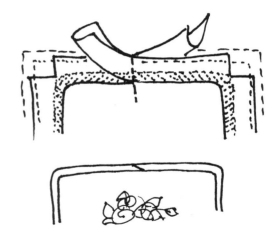

— Cut a bias strip the length around the cushion x 4 cm ($1^3/_5$″) plus 10 cm (4″).
— Fold and machine the bias over the piping cord, using a standard machine foot.
— Pin piping onto the cushion front, commencing at the middle of any side. Taper the cord from the seam allowance into the sewing line and pin to the corner.
— Place one cut through the turnings of the bias at the corner point, to allow the cord to neatly turn the corner.
— Continue around all sides and taper out at the end. The cord ends, not the covering bias, can be cut off at the same position.

— Machine cord into position with the standard machine foot.
— Pin back of cushion to the front using the machine line on the back, which is holding the piping in place, as a guide.
— Undo the zip slightly.
— Using a zip foot, machine around the cushion, pressing hard against the piped cord.
— Turn cushion to the right side.

To Frill Edge

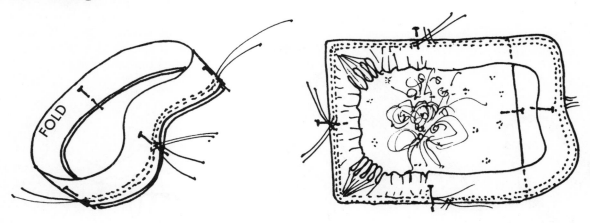

A cushion may be finished with just a frill or a piping can be used in conjunction with a frill. Using a frill and piping together is a good idea if you want to highlight the colours used in the appliqué.

You will need a strip of fabric one and a half times the length around the cushion x 18 cm (7$\frac{1}{5}$"").
— Sew strips together to form a circle, iron and fold in half lengthways.
— Divide the circle into quarters and mark the positions with a pin.
— Machine sew two rows of gathering in each quarter.
— Divide each side of the cushion front in half and mark with a pin.
— Match each quarter of frill to each quarter of cushion.
— Pull up gathering stitch until the frill fits the cushion. Most of the gathering should be in the corners, to allow the frill to turn the corner without the outside edge rolling in.
— Machine on the frill, sewing on the outside row of gathering.

— Fold over and pin the frill down at the corners, to prevent the frill being caught in the final row of machining.
— Pin the back cushion onto the front of the cushion, with right sides together.
— Make sure the zip is slightly undone.
— Machine from the front, inside the row of machining showing. This final row of machining should be in the centre of the two rows of gathering on the frill.
— Turn cushion to the right side. Check to see the frill is not caught, then pull out the row of gathering showing.

To Ruche Edge

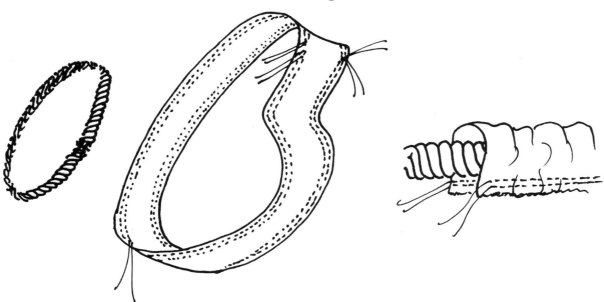

A ruched edge is very similar to a frilled edge except that it is narrower and padded with either a soft thick cord or a roll of wadding (padding). Like the frill it can be used in conjunction with piping.

You will need a strip of fabric one and a half times the length around the cushion x 12 cm (4⅘"). You will also need a thick, soft, prewashed cord or roll of wadding, the length around the cushion plus 15 cm (6").
— Join the ends of the strip to form a circle.
— Join the ends of the cord to form a circle (this is smaller than the fabric circle).
— Machine two rows of gathering on each side of fabric circle.

— Fold the sides of the fabric circle over the cord and pull up to fit the cord.
— Machine both edges of the ruching fabric together.
— Attach the ruching to the cushion in the same manner as described for the frill (page 57).
— Do not iron the ruched edge.

FINISHING

A cushion insert is used to fill the cushion. This can be made or bought. The insert should be 2 cm (¾″) larger than the cushion cover to give a well-filled appearance.

Put the padded insert inside the cushion and zip up, making sure the padding rounds the cushion smoothly.

FIRESCREEN

The firescreen was made using the wreath design from the quilt and a small design carried into the side panels.

REQUIREMENTS

- Tone on tone printed background fabric, the same size as the central panel of the quilt (see page 46) and side panels.
- Small pieces of printed fabrics for flowers and leaves.
- Two values of the same colour for ribbons and bow.
- Threads to match.
- Wadding (padding).
- Frame — the frame illustrated was made to order.

METHOD

1. Cut out background fabric.

2. Transfer designs onto background fabrics (for wreath page 34, for side panels page 36).

3. Work appliqué design as suggested in chapter Appliqué Techniques (page 8).

4. If a three-dimensional effect is desired, some of the petals can be padded. Stitch three-quarters of the petal and ease a small amount of wadding under the petal, then complete the hemming. Be careful not to use too much padding as the background fabric can become distorted, which makes it hard to get a smooth finish when stretched on the board within the frame.

5. To assemble the screen, firstly iron the appliqué from the wrong side on a soft towel. Place wadding (padding) in place. Align the centre of the design with the centre of the backing board. Fold the fabric over to the back and staple to the backing board.

ALTERNATIVE USE OF PATTERNS

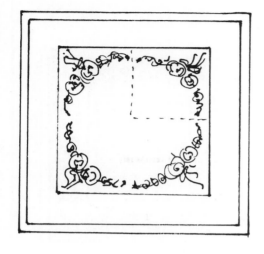

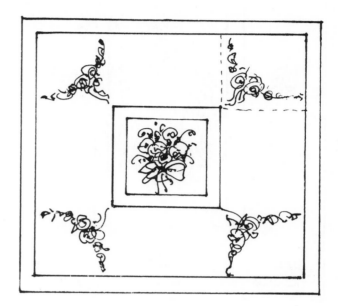

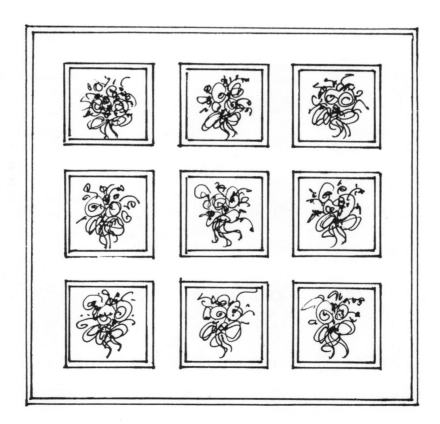

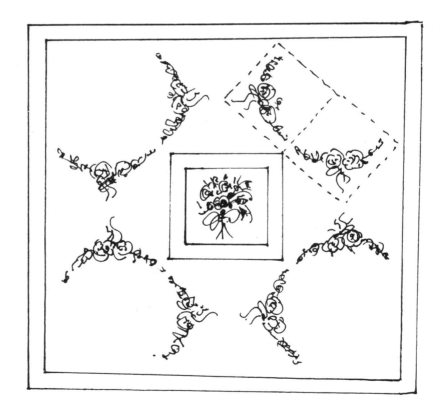

To "all y'all"

For those of you who have visited, this
is a reminder. For those of you who haven't,
hopefully you will get a chance to to check
things out for yourselves.

... Remember, we'd like to see
you all, anytime!

The Hildebrands.

DALLAS FORT WORTH

A Picture Book to Remember Her by

CRESCENT BOOKS
NEW YORK

They call it a "metroplex," and it has become America's eighth most-populated urban center. But the marriage of Dallas and Fort Worth has never been smooth. A dozen years ago, they were separated by a gulf of dry, black land. Today they are joined by suburbs known as the Mid-Cities and, as often happens in a marriage, these children of theirs are drawing them closer together even if there is still very little love lost in the process.

Dallas is not at all what people in other parts of America think it is. Even though it was once home to gamblers and dance hall girls and an outlaw or two, today's gamblers take their plunges in Wall Street and the girls who go dancing on weekends go to work in conservative business suits all week long. If there are outlaws, there are more banks for them to rob and more lawyers to defend them in Dallas than in almost any other city in the United States.

Fort Worth, on the other hand, is quite close to what outsiders think Dallas is. You're more likely to get a good chicken-fried steak there and there are more pickup trucks on its streets.

They're more relaxed about life in Fort Worth and, though they are beginning to get their own glass and stainless steel skyscrapers and high-rise hotels, they still like to think of themselves as a Cowtown. Exactly the image Dallas would like to erase.

A first-time visitor once asked an old-time Dallasite where to find "the real Dallas." He was directed to a construction site. But unlike its rival for bigness and greatness, Houston, it does all it can to project an image of sophistication and stability. And though they can't help swaggering a bit – they are super-achievers after all – they do maintain an air of upper-class elegance.

The Dallas image has been roughened up a bit in recent years by a television soap opera that seems to tell the world that Dallasites are likely to lie and cheat and connive a lot. With more than three million people packed into its 55-mile-wide urban area, there probably are some people who sit around their swimming pools in silk robes and Stetson hats scheming about getting richer or getting even. Even though Dallas people are more like the rest of America's population than the TV view suggests.

But people in Dallas don't seem to mind. Its Mayor said of it: "If they wanted a really Western city, they should have called it 'Fort Worth,' but I guess they wanted a city with a reputation for money, and Dallas has that."

The divisions between the two cities have dwindled thanks to the growth of the cities between them. People in Fort Worth aren't ashamed to run over to Dallas to root for the home-town football team, the Cowboys; and folks from Dallas don't mind having to go to Tarrant County, of which Fort Worth is the County Seat, to watch the Texas Rangers play baseball. People who live in Mid-Cities towns like Arlington say they like the choice of being able to go either way. But many of them, of course, are newcomers to the Sun Belt and don't have the old prejudices.

The rivalry goes back to the very beginning, when Dallas and Fort Worth were arguing over which was to be the more major stop on the Texas and Pacific Railroad, which finally pushed through in 1876. In Fort Worth, local citizens volunteered personally to grade 26 miles of roadbed, an offer the railroad gratefully accepted. But the job had to be done before the legislature adjourned for the year and its land grant subsidy ran out. They did it and got their railroad. But over in Dallas, they got the railroad with less work by simply attaching an innocent-sounding rider to a bill in the legislature that the new line should cross the Houston and Texas Central Railroad "within one mile of Browder Springs." The legislators in Austin didn't know that Browder Springs was in Dallas and, assuming that it was a convenience to the railroad to take on water there, passed the bill and went home. By the time they found out it was too late to do anything about it and the Great State of Texas found out what it was up against with the Great City of Dallas.

In the years between, rivalry between Dallas and Fort Worth reached an almost fevered pitch. In 1873 a visitor from Dallas wrote a letter to a local newspaper saying that Fort Worth was so dead that he saw a panther asleep in the middle of the main street and no people anywhere near to do anything about it.

Dallasites laughed. But in Fort Worth, the local fire department adopted a panther cub as its mascot and dozens of local clubs changed their names to include the word "panther." From that moment, they told the world, Fort Worth was "panther city."

Now they call themselves part of a "Metroplex." And even by Texas standards, the combination of Dallas and Fort Worth is a wonder to behold. It's an amazing combination of East and West... proof that the twain can meet and the result can be good.

Facing page: The Texas flag in front of the Thanks-Giving Tower.

Previous pages: (top left) the Hyatt Regency
Hotel, (bottom left) Palm Restaurant, (right)
downtown Dallas. Facing page: (top) the mirrored
facade of the Hyatt Regency Hotel, (bottom)
downtown Dallas viewed from Continental Avenue.
Top left: the Reunion Tower, (top) the buildings
surrounding Thanks-Giving Square, (above and left)
Municipal Plaza Park.

Previous pages: (top and bottom right) downtown Dallas at night, (top left) an aerial view of the city, (bottom left) the InterFirst Bank building dominates the view from the southeast. Old City Park (these pages) contains restored or rebuilt buildings in their pioneer state, as well as Browder Springs, the water source that brought the railroad to Dallas.

Top: an aerial view of the Dallas skyline, (left) part of the new Market Center complex, (above) view across Thanks-Giving Square. Facing page: an aerial view of the Market Center (top), and Las Colinas Urban Center (bottom), a multi-faceted development located west of Dallas. Overleaf: (left) Reunion Tower, and (right) Ervay St.

Views of Thanks-Giving Square: (above and top) the water gardens and (left) the chapel in front of Thanks-Giving Tower. Facing page: (top left) the Hyatt Regency Hotel, (top right) Thanks-Giving Tower and (bottom) a courtyard along the side of Arco Tower. Overleaf: (and center inset) Historical Plaza featuring the Bryan Cabin. Insets: (left) J.F.Kennedy Memorial and (right) looking east toward Houston St.

The InterFirst Bank building towers over Historical Plaza (below) and the Railway Co. building (bottom right). Bottom left: the Hyatt Regency Hotel with the Reunion Tower (right). Facing page: (top) the city viewed from Municipal Plaza Park and (bottom) at dusk, from the southwest. Overleaf: the glamorous new Lincoln Center at sunset.

evious pages: Municipal Plaza (right and top ft),and a view of New City Hall (bottom left) owing the illuminated Reunion Tower. Facing ge: the Dallas skyline viewed from (top) unicipal Plaza and (bottom) Convention Plaza. Top d above: Texas State Fair Park, setting for the citing fair held each October.

Above: the War Memorial in front of the Convention Center. Overleaf: axis deer at the International Wildlife Park between Dallas and Fort Worth which also features eland antelope (inset top), zebra (center left), African elephant (center right), wildebeest (bottom right) and scimitar oryx (bottom left).

Previous pages: the famous Southfork Ranch, used in the T.V. soap opera *Dallas*. These pages and overleaf: one of the two White Water parks between Dallas and Fort Worth, featuring exciting attractions such as the Spanish galleon (above), wave pool (facing page top) and the new Black Hole (top) – a tubular helter-skelter.

Previous pages: the Six Flags Over Texas
amusement park is ranked as Texas' top tourist
attraction. It is viewed here from the park's
own observation tower. These pages: aerial views
of the Wet n'Wild water park.

Overleaf: looking west, over Interstate 30
towards Fort Worth, where, as the sophisticated
skyline shows, one finds modern development side
by side with the origins of the Wild West.
Insets show: (top left) the Casa Manana theater
and (bottom) the Kimbell Museum art gallery,
features of Fort Worth's Cultural District. Top
right: the Fort Worth Water Gardens.

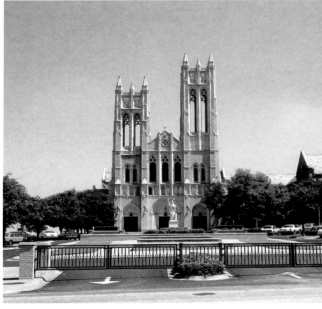

Previous pages: Main St., looking north over the
Texan Lone Star motif. This page (top) Six Flags
Over Texas amusement park, between Dallas and For
Worth. Remaining pictures show Fort Worth's mixtur
of ancient and modern architecture, with the First
Methodist Church (above) and the Tarrant Conventi
Center (facing page top). Overleaf: the restored
area at the north end of Main St.

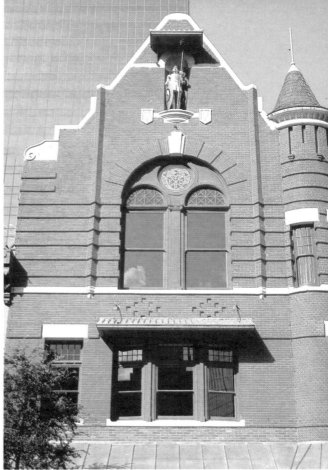

This page: some of the restored buildings on Main St. and (top left) Commerce St. Facing page: (top) a small square on Main St., (bottom) the water gardens on Commerce St. Overleaf: the beautiful Fort Worth Japanese Garden. Insets show from left to right: the Koi fish (Imperial Carp), the Meditation Garden and the entrance gate.

Previous page: shady trees balance the ultra-modern design of a small square on Main St. These pages: views of the skyline from east of the city. Overleaf: an impressive aerial view of downtown Fort Worth, with insets highlighting (center left) the Tarrant Convention Center and (far right) the Hyatt Regency Hotel on Main St.

Previous pages: (main picture and center inset left) views of the futuristic Tarrant Convention Center. Right inset: dense foliage conceals the Trinity River, which runs through downtown Fort Worth. Left inset: the Amon G. Carter Jr. Exhibits Hall, part of the Amon Carter Museum located in the Cultural District. Named after the newspape publisher and philanthropist Amon G. Carter Sr., who collected works embodying the pioneer spirit, it is one of the foremost museums of American art. These pages: more examples of Fort Worth's varied architecture. Overleaf: the Tarrant Convention Center dominates an aerial view.